ROCK CYCLE

Kirsten Larson

Rourke
Educational Media

rourkeeducationalmedia.com

*Scan for Related Titles and
Teacher Resources*

Before Reading:

Building Academic Vocabulary and Background Knowledge

Before reading a book, it is important to tap into what your child or students already know about the topic. This will help them develop their vocabulary, increase their reading comprehension, and make connections across the curriculum.

1. *Look at the cover of the book. What will this book be about?*
2. *What do you already know about the topic?*
3. *Let's study the Table of Contents. What will you learn about in the book's chapters?*
4. *What would you like to learn about this topic? Do you think you might learn about it from this book? Why or why not?*
5. *Use a reading journal to write about your knowledge of this topic. Record what you already know about the topic and what you hope to learn about the topic.*
6. *Read the book.*
7. *In your reading journal, record what you learned about the topic and your response to the book.*
8. *After reading the book complete the activities below.*

Content Area Vocabulary

Read the list. What do these words mean?

buoyant
collide
convection
dense
deposited
erosion
hypothesis
igneous rock
magma
metamorphic rocks
observation
processes
sediment
sedimentary rock
weathering

After Reading:

Comprehension and Extension Activity

After reading the book, work on the following questions with your child or students in order to check their level of reading comprehension and content mastery.

1. *How did James Hutton change the way people thought about Earth?* (Summarize)
2. *How do rocks help scientists determine the age of the planet?* (Infer)
3. *What can rocks tell you about the place they're found?* (Asking questions)
4. *What are the rocks like where you live?* (Text to self connection)
5. *Why is it important for scientists to study tectonic plates?* (Asking questions)

Extension Activity

Start a rock collection. Look for various types of rocks around your home, school, and other places you visit. Design a box or board to display the rocks, and include information about each one. You can also create a virtual rock collection at www.learner.org/interactives/rockcycle/types.html.

Table of Contents

READING ROCKS

In the late 1700s, most scientists believed that planet Earth was very young—no more than 6,000 years old. They thought a great flood once shaped the land. But one man thought differently.

James Hutton believed natural **processes** formed and continued to form the Earth over long periods of time. He thought immense heat deep inside Earth pushed up the land to form new mountains.

James Hutton
1726 – 1797

Over millions of years, weather eroded the layers of soft and hard rock of Monument Valley, a desert region on the Arizona-Utah border.

Over time, wind, rain, and other forces wore down the Earth. Some of this mud and sand became new rock, and the cycle started again. According to Hutton, this cycle of building up and breaking down over and over took much longer than 6,000 years.

Old as the Hills!

Jack Hills in Western Australia is home to the oldest pieces of Earth ever found. Bits of the mineral zircon 4.4 billion years old were discovered among the rocks.

To prove his **hypothesis**, Hutton and two other scientists traveled by boat down the coast of Scotland hunting for rocks to tell the story. At Siccar Point on the North Sea, the men found a unique formation. At the bottom was gray, layered rock, like a layered birthday cake. But the layers of this rock had been turned on their sides. They stood straight up and down.

Siccar Point is now considered the most important geological location in the world.

To Hutton, this proved that powerful forces had made the layers crash, turn, and shoot up out of the ocean where they had formed. On top of the vertical rocks was another slab of gray rock, and then another layer of newer red rock. Since Hutton knew how long it took mud to build up in rivers, he concluded Siccar Point must have taken hundreds of thousands of years to form.

Hutton published his findings in the 1780s. Scientists of the day were slow to accept his ideas, especially his suggestion that Earth was very old. Today Hutton's theories are the basis of the study of geology. Many experts consider him the father of geology and the rock cycle.

Geological Time

Rock layers, called strata, are used by scientists to determine the relative ages of events and objects in Earth's history. The Permian through Jurassic strata in the Colorado Plateau area of southeastern Utah show how scientists represent Earth's geologic time vertically, since new rock can only be laid upon older rock.

7

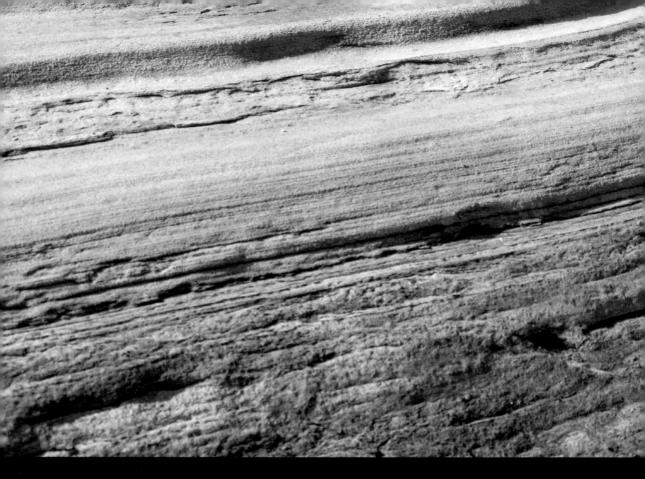

RECYCLING ROCKS

As Hutton discovered, rocks are not created from nothing nor ever completely destroyed. Instead, they are recycled over and over again through a process called the rock cycle. Think of rocks as glass jars. When you send an empty jar to a recycling factory, the glass is crushed into little pieces. Then it's melted down and poured into molds to harden and form new containers. The glass is not created nor destroyed during the process, it just changes form.

The rock cycle works in much the same way. Rain, wind, and other forces wear down old rocks. The rock fragments are **deposited** in layers by wind and water over long periods of time. The weight of

There are three basic types of sedimentary rocks: clastic, chemical, and organic.

many layers squeezes them and cements them together, creating sedimentary rocks. Through heat and pressure, the chemical makeup of any rock can change. These are called **metamorphic rocks**. If the rock melts during the process, it becomes the raw material for **igneous rock**. These are rocks that form **magma**, or molten rock.

Rockin' Makeovers

The name for metamorphic rocks comes from the word metamorphosis. It means a complete change in appearance or makeup. Metamorphosis happens at temperatures between 480 degrees Fahrenheit (250 degrees Celsius) and 1,290 degrees Fahrenheit (700 degrees Celsius). At those temperatures, the rocks do not melt.

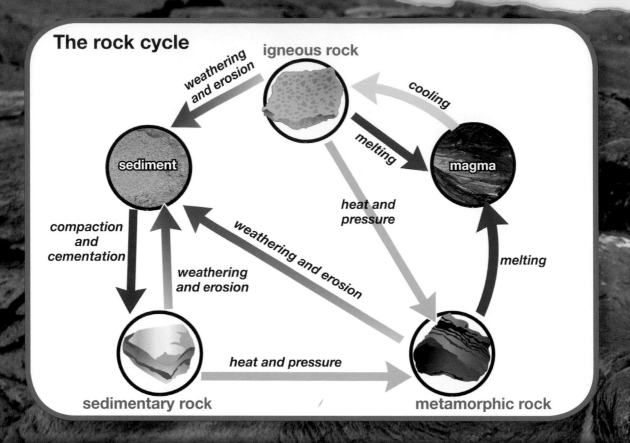

The rock cycle

- weathering and erosion
- igneous rock
- cooling
- sediment
- melting
- magma
- heat and pressure
- compaction and cementation
- weathering and erosion
- weathering and erosion
- melting
- sedimentary rock
- heat and pressure
- metamorphic rock

To understand how rocks form and break down, we have to understand what happens underneath Earth's surface. Our planet is not the same throughout. Instead, it is like an onion, made of layers. These layers were created when Earth was a brand new planet.

Scientists think a Mars-sized object hit the Earth soon after it formed. The explosion would have been as powerful as a trillion nuclear bombs, causing a chunk of Earth to break off and form the moon. Earth's crust melted from the impact, and a magma ocean covered the planet. Because the outer layer of the planet was liquid, heavier chunks sunk to the middle and formed the core. Meanwhile, lighter rock drifted to the surface and formed the crust as the planet cooled. Today, Earth has three main layers: the crust, the mantle, and the core.

Tough on the Outside

Both the crust and the upper part of the mantle, the layer below the crust, are strong and hard. Together, these solid parts of Earth are known as the lithosphere. The lithosphere is about 62 miles (100 kilometers) thick.

outer core

inner core

mantle

crust

Magma is produced when high pressure combine with high temperatures, causing rocks in the area to melt.

crust

mantle

outer core

inner core

Earth's Layers

Mantle: Too Hot to Handle

Near the crust, the temperature of the mantle is about 1,800 degrees Fahrenheit (1,000 degrees Celsius). Closer to the core, it can be 6,700 degrees Fahrenheit (3,700 degrees Celsius).

The crust is the outermost layer. It's what you stand on at the park or at the beach. Like an onion's papery skin, the crust is very thin, stretching down only about 25 miles (40 kilometers). Under the ocean, the crust is even thinner, only about 5 miles (8 kilometers) deep. Much of the rocks in the crust are basalt and granite, which

Making Waves

To learn about Earth's lithosphere, scientists create seismic waves, the same type of waves earthquakes make. Sometimes they use explosives to create the waves. Once the waves start, they time how fast the waves move through the rock and note if they bounce back. From that information, scientists learn about the types of rock in the mantle.

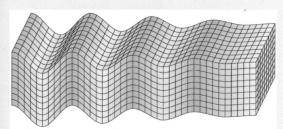

Recordings of seismic waves from earthquakes led to the discovery of the Earth's core.

Below the crust is the mantle, which makes up most of the Earth. The rocks of the mantle are more **dense**. The closer you get to the core, the hotter and denser the rocks become. Some rocks in the mantle melt, turning into magma. Though the mantle is not liquid, it flows like honey or hot tar.

The core is the heavy center of the planet, made of mostly iron and nickel. The outer portion of the core is hot and liquid, while the inner core remains solid like a peach pit. You would have to drill down 1,800 miles (2,900 kilometers) to reach the core. That's about the distance from Los Angeles, California, to Chicago, Illinois.

INSIDE THE EARTH

Examining a book of maps in 1910, German Alfred Wegener noticed the east coast of South America seemed to fit into the west coast of Africa like a jigsaw puzzle. Other scientists made this **observation** almost 300 years before, but they had no way of proving the hypothesis. Wegener, a weather scientist by training, set out to find proof.

Alfred Wegener
1880 – 1930

He discovered fossils and rocks on both continents that were similar. He also studied plants and animals found on the two continents and noted similarities. Could these two hunks of land have been joined together years ago?

before

after

14

Wegener's research proved that all the land on Earth was once one giant landmass. He called it Pangea, meaning *all land*. Wegener theorized that over time, Pangea broke up. Hunks of land drifted apart to form the continents we have today, a theory known as continental drift. Fifty years later, scientists began to understand the forces that drive continental drift: plate tectonics.

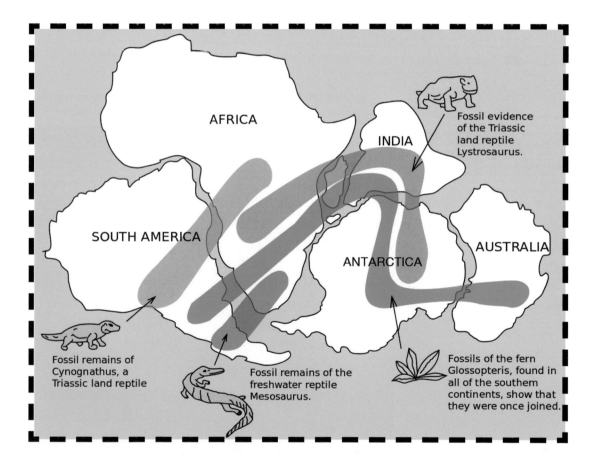

AFRICA

INDIA

Fossil evidence of the Triassic land reptile Lystrosaurus.

SOUTH AMERICA

ANTARCTICA

AUSTRALIA

Fossil remains of Cynognathus, a Triassic land reptile

Fossil remains of the freshwater reptile Mesosaurus.

Fossils of the fern Glossopteris, found in all of the southern continents, show that they were once joined.

Drilling for Discovery

Some scientists have tried to drill to the mantle to see the rocks up close. So far no one has been successful. In 2012, a Japanese science team drilled down 1.5 miles (2.5 kilometers) below the seafloor.

The Earth's hard lithosphere is broken up into plates that fit together. These plates shift and move very slowly, so slowly that you often don't feel it at all.

Places where plates move away from each other are called divergent boundaries. The lithosphere stretches, thins out, and eventually breaks. It's like blowing a giant bubble with chewing gum until it pops. When the lithosphere snaps, magma rises up and cools, forming new crust. The island of Iceland, for example, has grown an average of one inch (2.5 centimeters) each year as the North American and Eurasian plates move away from each other.

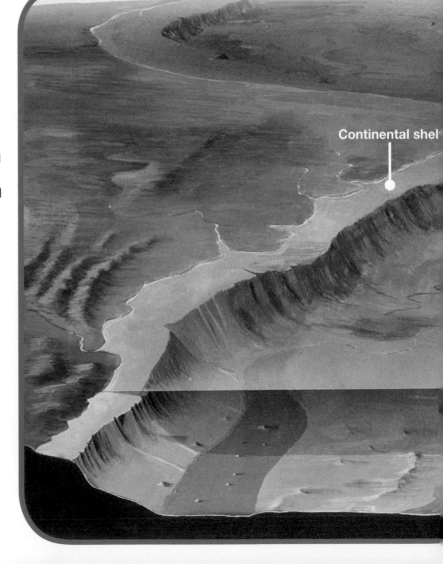

Continental shelf

Earth's ocean floors are constantly in motion, spreading from the center and sinking at the edges. Seafloor spreading is not consistent at all mid-ocean ridges. Slowly spreading ridges feature tall, narrow cliffs and mountains. Rapidly spreading ridges have gentler slopes.

Crash Course

When two plates collide, the plate with less dense rocks rises to the top. This plate is more **buoyant**, like an air-filled beach ball. The plate with more dense rocks sinks like a ball made of heavy iron. Continental plates are more buoyant than ocean plates. When the two collide, they end up on top.

- Trench
- Oceanic Crust
- Lithosphere
- Asthenosphere
- Volcanoes
- Continental Crust
- Magma
- Lithosphere
- Asthenosphere

Transform fault

Ocean trench

Ocean ridge

Volcano

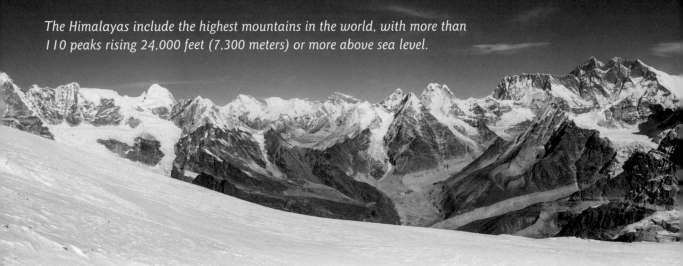

The Himalayas include the highest mountains in the world, with more than 110 peaks rising 24,000 feet (7,300 meters) or more above sea level.

In some places, plates **collide** at convergent boundaries. One plate comes out on top, while the other is forced down below, where the rock can be melted and recycled. The uppermost plate may buckle, building mountains like the Himalayas in Asia or volcanoes like those that formed the Andes Mountains in South America. When two ocean plates collide, deep ocean trenches and volcanic islands can form like the Mariana Islands, a chain of 14 volcanic islands in the Pacific.

In other places, the plates move past each other, forming earthquakes. These are called transform boundaries. California's famed San Andreas Fault lies along the area where the North American Plate and Pacific Plate slip past each other.

Transform plate boundary

Convergent plate boundary

Set in Motion

Scientists also wonder how the motions of the plates first started. No one knows for sure, but Dr. Vicki Hansen has a hypothesis. She thinks comets or asteroids bombarded the Earth 2.5 billion years ago. The devastating impacts allowed magma to seep onto Earth's surface, starting plate tectonics.

What keeps the plates moving? Scientists are still studying this.
Convection currents in the mantle play a major role. Imagine the
melted mantle is a large pot of water on the stove. The water right
above the flame warms up the fastest. As it heats up, the water
becomes more buoyant, like a hot air balloon, and floats to the top.
New, cooler water takes its place at the bottom of the pot. As water
heats up and rises then cools and sinks, it creates a circular current,
called a convection current. This is similar to what happens in the
mantle. Circular heating and cooling of the mantle helps carry the
plates, like a car's
wheels drive it from
place to place.

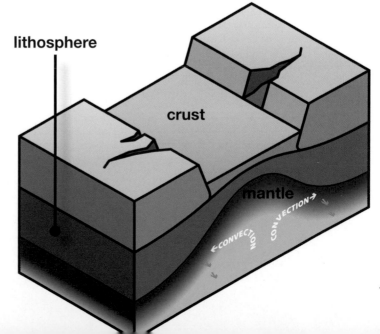

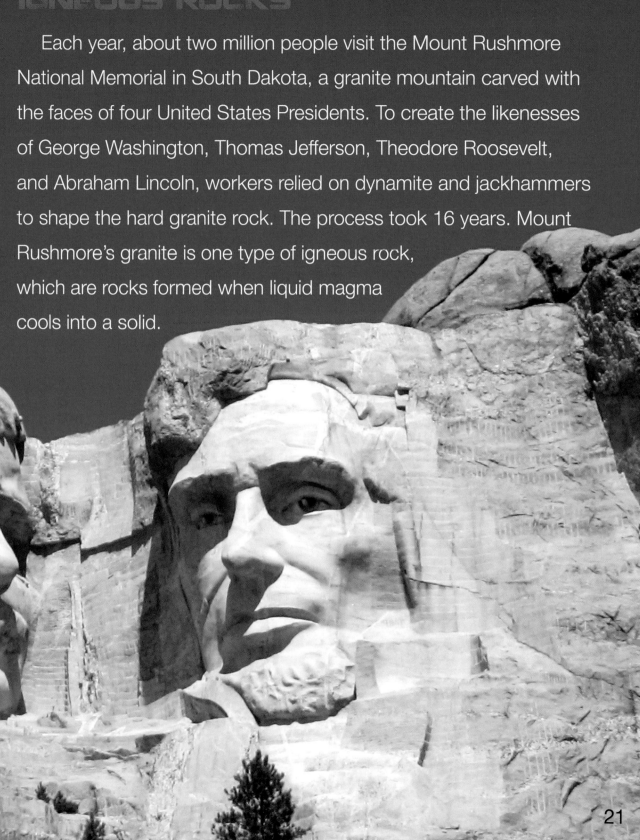

Each year, about two million people visit the Mount Rushmore National Memorial in South Dakota, a granite mountain carved with the faces of four United States Presidents. To create the likenesses of George Washington, Thomas Jefferson, Theodore Roosevelt, and Abraham Lincoln, workers relied on dynamite and jackhammers to shape the hard granite rock. The process took 16 years. Mount Rushmore's granite is one type of igneous rock, which are rocks formed when liquid magma cools into a solid.

Lava vs. Magma

What's the difference between magma and lava? They are both melted rock. The difference is in where you find it. Magma is the name for molten rock when it's deep inside Earth. When that melted rock breaks through and erupts from a volcano, it is called lava.

One type of igneous rock forms when magma reaches Earth's surface either through volcanoes or cracks in the Earth's crust. Some volcanoes form where two plates collide, and one plate is pushed down into the mantle. There the rock melts, creating magma. The magma is hotter and less dense than the surrounding rock. It rises up and forces its way to the surface. When this happens, look out!

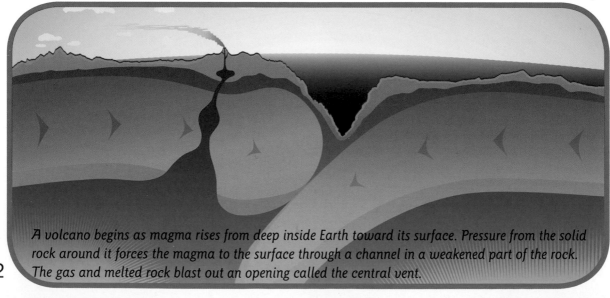

A volcano begins as magma rises from deep inside Earth toward its surface. Pressure from the solid rock around it forces the magma to the surface through a channel in a weakened part of the rock. The gas and melted rock blast out an opening called the central vent.

Sometimes the magma flows up through one central vent, like Mount Saint Helens in Washington. Its violent eruption sent rock and ash 60,000 feet (18,300 meters) into the sky–twice as high as airplanes fly. Or lava can ooze more slowly down the side of a volcano, as it does on Mauna Loa on the Big Island in Hawaii. This process has built Mauna Loa into the largest mountain on Earth when measured to the seafloor. It's even taller than Mount Everest!

Other eruptions are more like cracks that allow lava to pour out, called fissure eruptions. These occur where ocean plates move away from each other. In 1783, a fissure eruption in Iceland measured 20 miles (32 kilometers) long!

Ring of Fire

For years scientists noticed a ring of volcanoes in the Pacific Ocean. Known as the Ring of Fire, the area is home to 90 percent of the world's earthquakes and most of its active volcanoes. The ring traces the outline of the Pacific Plate, which collides with or slips past several other plates.

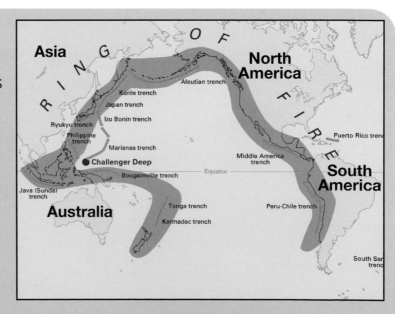

Other igneous rocks form when volcanoes toss lava into the air, where it cools quickly, making fine-grained rocks. Obsidian and pumice are two types of rock that form this way. People ground up pumice for early toothpastes. They used obsidian for arrowheads and spear points.

pumice

obsidian

Sometimes magma doesn't make it to Earth's surface. Instead, it stays underground. Because the magma cools more slowly there, the rock's crystals can grow quite large. The result is a coarse-grained rock with large, visible crystals, like the granite of Mount Rushmore. These rocks stay hidden underground until the rock above it wears away.

Extrusive vs. Intrusive

Extrusive rocks form when magma reaches Earth's surface, usually through a volcano. When the rocks form deep inside Earth's crust, they are known as intrusive igneous rocks.

intrusive igneous rocks

The T. Rex discovered in 1988 in Montana is one of about half a dozen nearly complete T. Rex skeletons that have been uncovered. It is displayed in the Smithsonian Museum of Natural History.

SEDIMENTARY ROCKS

In 2000, paleontologist Bob Harmon took his lunch break. He and his team were digging for dinosaur bones in an area of **sedimentary rock** in eastern Montana.

All of a sudden, Harmon glimpsed a giant bone poking out from a rock wall–a T. Rex leg bone. It was so big, scientists had to break open the bone before a helicopter could fly it to the lab. That broken bone led to an amazing find: the first soft tissue of a 68-million-year-old dinosaur. Most scientists believed an animal's soft parts couldn't survive millions of years. But they were wrong. Scientists now are studying dinosaur blood vessels and cells. Only sedimentary rock could have yielded such a find.

A Blast from the Past

When plants or animals die and are buried by sediment, they may become fossils. Fossils have a greater chance of forming when the plant or animal is buried quickly in sand or soil before it can decay.

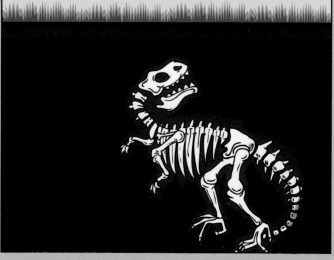

Rock layers formed during the Paleozoic Era are the most conspicuous in the Grand Canyon's walls.

Sedimentary rocks form from pieces of other rocks, known as **sediment**. Though rocks seem very hard, they have weak spots. If you hit one in just the right way, a rock can crack and break along these weak areas. Over time, even the hardest rocks break down through the actions of wind, water, chemicals, and other processes. This process, called **weathering**, often is driven by what its name suggests–the weather over long periods of time.

Physical weathering breaks rocks into smaller pieces that have the same chemical makeup as the original rock. This can happen when water from rain, rivers, or melted snow seeps into small cracks and freezes. The ice expands and breaks up the rock. Other times, wind and water pick up and carry away small pieces of rock. Once rocks begin to break down, the broken bits are more easily transported away through the process of **erosion**.

Activity

Create Your Own Caves

The weathering action of water carves dramatic caves and sinkholes in rocks like limestone. This karst topography is common in places such as Mexico's Yucatan peninsula, Kentucky, and Florida.

What You'll Need

- 10 or more sugar cubes
- water
- food coloring
- measuring cup
- eyedropper
- baking sheet

What You'll Do

1. On the baking sheet, stack up your sugar cubes any way you like.
2. In the measuring cup, add a few drops of food coloring to 1/4 cup (60 milliliters) water.
3. Using the eyedropper, drip the water onto the sugar to simulate the action of water dissolving limestone.
4. Observe the changes in the topography.
5. Repeat steps 3 and 4 until you make a hole all the way through the layers of sugar. What do you observe about the action of water on the sugar/limestone?

Another type of weathering, called chemical weathering, actually changes the rock's chemical makeup. A wrought-iron gate rusting is a form of chemical weathering. Oxygen dissolved in water combines with iron to create new chemicals, including what we know as rust.

Acid rain and the dry deposition of acidic particles contribute to the corrosion of metals and the deterioration of paint and stone.

Sometimes rainwater mixes with chemicals in the air creating acid rain. This acid can break down rocks like limestone and marble. In Washington, D.C., acid rain has damaged some of the national monuments. At the Jefferson Memorial, the detailed work on the columns has started to wear away.

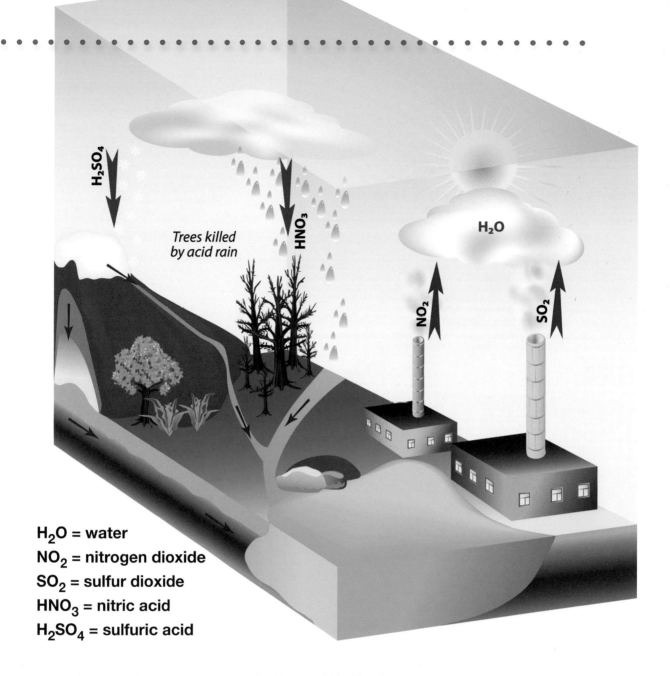

H₂SO₄

HNO₃

Trees killed by acid rain

H₂O

NO₂

SO₂

H_2O = water
NO_2 = nitrogen dioxide
SO_2 = sulfur dioxide
HNO_3 = nitric acid
H_2SO_4 = sulfuric acid

Plant Power

Plants help with weathering, too. Roots can grow into rocks, making holes larger and breaking them up.

Glaciers occupy about 10 percent of the world's total land area, with most located in polar regions like Antarctica, Greenland, and the Canadian Arctic.

Wind and water not only break down rock, but also carry rock away, a process called erosion. Imagine small pebbles carried downstream by a rushing river, or a windstorm picking up grains of sand. These are two ways bits of rocks are transported, but not the only ways. Glaciers, giant ice sheets, flow slowly downhill thanks to the tug of gravity. They are capable of carrying giant boulders along with them, which grind away at bedrock below the glacier. Gravity also pulls on rocks and mud causing rockslides and mudflows.

Nicolaus Steno
1638 – 1686

Layer by Layer

Danish scientist Nicolaus Steno was one of the first to study rock layers in the late 1700s. He realized that the pull of gravity caused layers of sediment to be deposited horizontally, like layers of a birthday cake. When rock layers are turned on their side, like at Siccar Point in Scotland, tectonic forces must have acted on the layers after they formed. Steno also developed the principle of superposition, which says if layered rocks have not been disturbed, the oldest rock layers are on the bottom, and the newest on the top.

But what happens when the river slows its flow, the wind stops blowing, or glaciers melt? The sediment, the bits of rock and sand, is deposited in layers. Over time, new layers are deposited like the ingredients of a sandwich, covering the old layers and pushing down on them. Pressure, heat, and chemical changes cause the rocks to harden into layered sedimentary rock, just like cooking and pressing a cheese sandwich turns it into something new.

METAMORPHIC ROCKS

In New York City, the famed Empire State Building stands 1,250 feet (381 meters) high, a mass of steel and stone. For 41 years, it was the tallest building in the world. How were architects able to build so high? Metamorphic rock. Thirty-eight feet (12 meters) under the building sits a layer of metamorphic rock called Manhattan schist. Schist forms from sedimentary rock, but through high temperatures and immense pressure, it changed into a new type of rock. The schist provides a sturdy foundation that anchors the Empire State Building and other New York City skyscrapers.

The schist under the Empire State Building was compressed under tremendously high pressure over 300 million years ago.

Both sedimentary and igneous rocks can become metamorphic rocks. All it takes is high temperature and lots of squeezing.

Central Park in Manhattan is one of the rare places in New York City where ancient bedrock mingles with modern life.

Recrystallization

When metamorphosis happens, the texture and chemical makeup of rocks changes. The rocks have many of the same minerals as the parent rocks. The minerals just rearrange themselves, a process called recrystallization.

Metamorphic rocks form in many different ways. Most of them develop when two of Earth's tectonic plates crash into each other. The high heat and pressure from the collision forms bands of metamorphic rock across large areas. In the Himalayas, the highest mountains in the world, the Indian and Eurasian plates ran into each other, creating metamorphic rocks.

Meteor Crater was blasted out of the surrounding sandstone about 50,000 years ago. The dry Arizona climate has kept it close to impact-fresh ever since. For years, America's geologists insisted that the crater was just another dead volcano.

In other cases, metamorphosis affects smaller areas. If a pocket of magma inside Earth encounters solid rock, the intense heat may change the old rock surrounding the magma. Other times, metamorphosis is very dramatic, like when a meteorite smacks into Earth. The heat and force of the impact changes the rock where the meteorite landed.

FAST FACT

Metamorphic rock also is found in the seafloor where tectonic plates pull away from each other. Water trickles into the cracks and heats up, where it causes chemical changes.

Metamorphic rocks can provide scientists with clues about how the tectonic plates move in certain areas. A rock can form many different types of metamorphic rock, depending upon the temperatures and amount of squeezing they encounter. At very low pressure and temperature, a sedimentary rock might become slate, which builders use to make roofs. At higher temperature and pressure, that same rock would form gneiss, another building material.

slate

gneiss

The Taj Mahal

When Indian Emperor Shah Jahan's favorite wife died, he built India's famed Taj Mahal to honor her. It took more than 20,000 workers 17 years to build the structure made of white marble, a metamorphic rock. The main building, which houses her tomb, was finished in 1648. Today, the Taj Mahal is considered one of the Seven Wonders of the World.

USGS scientist Cynthia Gardner gathers rock samples from the new growth on the dome of Mount St. Helens.

REAL LIFE ROCK STARS

People who study rocks and the rock cycle are called geologists. These real, live rock stars use what they know about the rock cycle in many ways. Dr. Dorothy Oehler, for example, has spent more than 20 years working in the oil industry. She studied satellite information from remote places such as the African interior. Carefully noting the rocks and formations, she would predict whether the locations would be good spots to drill for oil.

Fossil Fuels

Oil and coal are known as fossil fuels. When plants and animals die and are buried, they experience heat, squeezing, and chemical changes over millions of years. Under just the right conditions they can form fossil fuels used to power cars and heat homes.

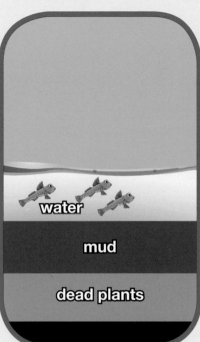

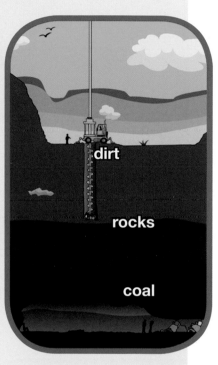

1. 300 million years ago, many giant plants died in swamps.

2. Over millions of years, the plant remains were buried under water and mud.

3. Ancient oceans dried up or receded. Heat and pressure turned the dead plants into coal.

Today, Oehler's work is a bit more out of this world. She's one of many scientists working with NASA's Curiosity Mars rover, a rolling robot on Mars.

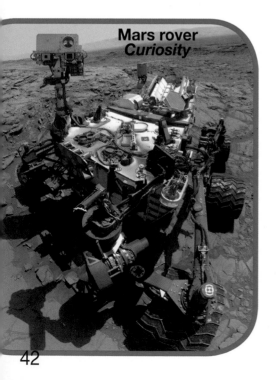

This photo was taken by NASA's Curiosity Mars rover. Scientists are using the rover to investigate how the environment on Mars changed billions of years ago.

Mars rover Curiosity

The rover's quest is to learn if Mars once had an environment that could support life. Oehler uses pictures the rover has taken, along with information from the rover's many science tools, to learn about Martian rocks. So far, the rocks have told scientists like Oehler that water once flowed on Mars. They also have found organic chemicals, the building blocks of life on Earth, in rocks on Mars.

Searching for Signs

Mars is not the only place in the solar system that scientists are searching for signs of life. On Saturn's moon Enceladus, a massive ocean lies beneath a frozen crust. Could it have been home to life? Scientists also are looking for clues on comets. In 2006, NASA found organic chemicals on the comet Wild 2. They wonder if a similar comet could have carried such chemicals to Earth.

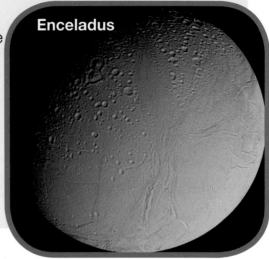

Enceladus

Earth is always changing, and rocks are too. Tectonic plates move and crash into each other. Sometimes they form mountains. Other times, one plate dives under another, rock melts forming magma. Magma from volcanoes and magma pools underground hardens to make igneous rocks.

Rocks may seem solid, but over time, all rocks break down into pebbles and fine grains of sand. Wind and water move these bits of rock, eventually dropping the sediment and forming sedimentary rocks with the help of pressure. Finally, high temperature and squeezing can turn any rock into metamorphic rock. Rocks are recycled over and over again, just as James Hutton first discovered all those years ago.

Chocolate Rock Cycle

You can replicate the rock cycle with tasty chocolate. Just make sure an adult is available to help you, since you'll use the microwave and a sharp grater.

What You'll Need

- squares of white and dark chocolate
- glass measuring cup
- oven mitts
- microwave oven
- aluminum foil
- dull knife
- grater
- heavy cans of food (like tomatoes)
- hand lens
- water

What You'll Do

1. Place a couple of squares of dark chocolate in the glass measuring cup and microwave on high power for about 10 seconds. Stir with knife. Repeat heating and stirring until chocolate is melted, just like magma. Use oven mitt to remove measuring cup from microwave.

2. Pour magma onto a sheet of foil and allow it to cool. Do not touch the hot chocolate! Once the chocolate has hardened, examine your chocolate igneous rock with the hand lens.

3. Remove rock from the foil and grate onto another sheet of foil, forming sediment. Grate white chocolate over top. Alternate layers of chocolate sediment.

4. Cover sediment with a layer of foil and stack heavy cans of food on top, to simulate the squeezing sedimentary rocks experience. Remove the top layer of foil and observe your sedimentary rock with a hand lens.

5. Heat about a half cup of water in the measuring cup for 30 seconds in the microwave. Use an oven mitt to remove. Cover sedimentary rock with foil and set the warm measuring cup on top for a couple of minutes to simulate metamorphosis.

6. Remove foil and observe your metamorphic rock. How is it different from the sedimentary rock?

So You Want to Be a Rock Star?

Geologists study rocks and the rock cycle, to learn about the planet's past, present, and future. Here are a few tips for breaking into the field of geology:

Study hard. Most geologists hold at least a bachelor's degree from a college or university, but many have master's degrees or doctorates.

Get comfortable with computers. Geologists use computers to analyze data, make maps, and create models.

Improve your outdoor skills. Many geologists perform fieldwork in remote places, which may involve camping and surviving in the wilderness.

Get some exercise. In the field, geologists might have to hike or climb many miles.

Make sure you have the right (write!) stuff. Geologists publish papers to share their finding with others. Your writing skills must be top notch.

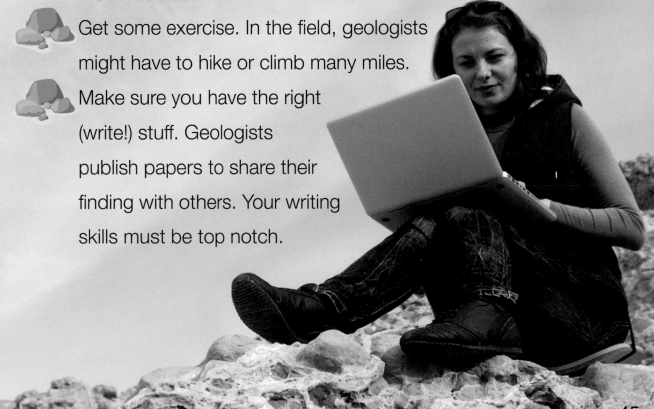

GLOSSARY

buoyant (BOI-uhnt): able to float

collide (kuh-LIDE): crash into each other

convection (kuhn-VEK-shuhn): circulation of heat, especially in air and liquids

dense (dens): heavy

deposited (di-PAH-zit-ed): laid down

erosion (i-ROH-zhuhn): the loosening of soils and rock so they can be moved

hypothesis (hye-PAH-thi-sis): a testable answer to a science question

igneous rock (IG-nee-uhs rahk): rock made from hardening magma

magma (MAG-muh): melted rock found inside the Earth

metamorphic rocks (met-uh-MOR-fik rahks): rocks that have changed because of squeezing and heat

observation (ahb-zur-VAY-shuhn): something a scientist notices by watching carefully

processes (PRAH-ses-es): a series of steps

sediment (SED-uh-muhnt): broken down rock and other fragments laid down by wind, water, and glaciers

sedimentary rock (sed-uh-MEN-tur-ee rahk): layered rock created when sediment is deposited and squeezed together

weathering (weth-ur-ing): the process of breaking down rocks into smaller rocks

INDEX

SHOW WHAT YOU KNOW

1. How did the layers of the Earth form?
2. What causes earthquakes and volcanoes?
3. Describe three ways igneous rocks can form.
4. Describe the forces that form the sediment that later becomes sedimentary rock.
5. In what ways is the rock cycle similar to recycling aluminum cans or glass bottles?

WEBSITES TO VISIT

http://kidsgeo.com/geology-for-kids/0025B-rock-cycle.php

www.mineralogy4kids.org/rock-cycle

https://eo.ucar.edu/kids/green/cycles8.htm

ABOUT THE AUTHOR

Kirsten W. Larson spent six years at NASA before writing for young people. She is the author of more than 16 books and a dozen articles about space potties, animal vampires, mammoth bones, and everything in between. She and her family live far too close to the San Andreas Fault in Southern California. Learn more at kirsten-w-larson.com.

Meet The Author!
www.meetREMauthors.com

© 2016 Rourke Educational Media

www.rourkeeducationalmedia.com

Cover and title page: volcano © Fotos593, cycle adapted from image © Andrei Marincas; page 4-5 © lightpix, page 5 map © pavalena; page 6 photo © dave souza at Wikipedia, page 7 map © Poligrafistka, rock © hsvrs; page 8-9 © SOUMITRA PENDSE, page 9 inset photo © kksteven, page 10 rock cycle adapted form illustration © Nerdist72, magma © Robert Crow'; page 12 illustration © Nick Hall, page 12-13 New York City © amriphoto, page 13 © Fouad A. Saad; page 15 globes © 253146733; page 16-17 © Designua, page 17 © Zern Liew; page 18-19 © Yongyut Kumsri, page 18 plate boundaries illustrations © Designua, page 19 © Zern Liew; page 20-21 © Francesco Dazzi; page 22 © volcano diagram © Andrea Danti, bottom diagram © daulon, page 23 photo © Harry Hu, volcano diagram © BlueRingMedia; page 24-25 © Wead, bottom left © dmitriyd, bottom right © joannawnuk; page 25 © johnandersonphoto; page 26-27 © David Herraez Calzada, page 27 © MarijaPiliponyte; page 28-29 © Ovidiu Hrubaru; page 31 © DomDew_Studio, page 31 diagram © Designua, photo © sevenke; page 32-33 © K_Boonnitrod; page 34-35 © Matej Kastelic, page 35 © Loadmaster (David R. Tribble); page 36-37 © David P. Smith; page 38 slate © marekuliasz, gneiss © www.sandatlas.org, page 39 © Sunny-s; page 40 courtesy of USGS, page 41 © debra hughes, NuConcept, Twinkie Artcat, Neyro, Photo Grafix Black Rhino Illustration; page 42 courtesy of NASA/JPL-Caltech/MSSS, page 43 courtesy of NASA/JPL/USGS; page 45 © shutterstock Image ID: 126195974, page 45 rock icon © Lightkite

Edited by: Keli Sipperley

Cover and Interior design by: Nicola Stratford   www.nicolastratford.com

Library of Congress PCN Data

Rock Cycle / Kirsten Larson
(Let's Explore Science)
ISBN 978-1-68191-398-8 (hard cover)
ISBN 978-1-68191-440-4 (soft cover)
ISBN 978-1-68191-479-4 (e-Book)
Library of Congress Control Number: 2015951565

Also Available as:

ROURKE'S e-Books

Printed in the United States of America, North Mankato, Minnesota